Reading for Personal Development

Reading for Personal Development

by Marta Merajver-Kurlat

Jorge Pinto Books Inc.
New York

Reading for Personal Development
Copyright © 2011 by Marta Merajver-Kurlat

All rights reserved. This book may not be reproduced in whole or in part, in any form (beyond copying permitted by Sections 107 and 108 of the United States Copyright Law, and except limited excerpts by reviewer for the public press), without written permission from Jorge Pinto Books Inc. 151 East 58th Street, New York, NY 10022.

Published by Jorge Pinto Books Inc., website: www.pintobooks.com
Cover design © 2011 by Nigel Holmes, website: www.nigelholmes.com
Book design by Charles King, website: www.ckmm.com

    ISBN13: 978-1-934978-58-0
    ISBN10: 1-934978-58-2

BIBLIOTREATMENT SERIES

This book is not intended as a replacement for professional medical, dietary, financial, or psychiatric assistance, if that is needed.

Contents

Introduction ix

Fyodor Dostoevsky: *Crime and Punishment* . . . 1

Aldous Huxley: *Brave New World* 9

Hermann Hesse: *Steppenwolf* 17

Juan Rulfo: *Pedro Páramo* 25

Sándor Márai: *Embers* 33

Miguel Ángel Asturias: *The President* 41

Giuseppe Tomasi di Lampedusa: *The Leopard* . . 49

Kazuo Ishiguro: *An Artist of the Floating World* . . 61

Margaret Atwood: *The Penelopiad* 71

Louis Bromfield: *Mr. Smith* 79

Introduction

This is the first book of a subseries included in *Bibliotreatment*. Reading is therapeutic, and many of the issues that may be worrying you have been broached by great writers whose insight sometimes makes you wonder whether you/someone you know have been spied on to provide literary material.

As a matter of fact, everything is a source of creativity for writers, and the coincidences we find between fictional lives and our own are simply due to the fact that the writer's raw material is human nature. Since the core of human nature is universal, we are bound to be looking at ourselves in a mirror when we pick great works.

A large number of educated people declare that they "don't read." This is not exactly true, since they do read a lot about their specific fields of activity. I guess that what is left out from their statement is the word "fiction." Thus, these non-fiction readers seem to be tacitly acknowledging a void in their daily practices.

I have often been told that reading with no practical goal in mind proves a waste of time, that it is a passive manner of entertainment suited only to those who do not feel the need to constantly meet and overcome challenges, and that the "imaginary worlds" of fiction can be effectively enjoyed by watching a movie, which takes less time and does not require building mental pictures of the content.

A large number of people do not seem to be aware that every life is a narrative. It could be said that experiences consist of two steps. In step one you play an active part. You are, so to speak, an actor improvising in a play without a script, for no two situations will ever be identical. In step two, you recall and retell what you lived. You do not perform these experiences again for others to watch, so you resort to linguistic and cohesive devices, filling in the gaps caused by forgotten chunks with plausible content to convey meaning. You have now become a narrator. In the long run, because your discourse covers many more subjects than those lying within your direct experience, the time you spend as a narrator exceeds by far the time you spend as an actor.

A third step indirectly results from the first two. When you interact with others, you will necessarily listen to their narratives. Since gap filling constitutes a fictional resource, it turns out that fiction has caught up with you even if you do not recognize it because it is not encased in a book.

Despite a widespread belief to the contrary, reading is not a passive but an extremely demanding interactive process. It "involves mental activity, is embedded in other communication abilities, and converts graphic stimuli into meaning."* Moreover, fiction works pose very real challenges. You need to pierce through the level of the enunciated (the actual words used and their arrangement in sentences) to reach the level of enunciation (to put it simply, what lies behind the words; what the author conveys even when she is not aware of actually having meant what seems patent to you). Between-the-lines reading is a fascinating exercise in detection, association, comparison, identification, debate, and much more.

Reading fiction is a manner of entertainment. We pick up a book to enter other worlds, to peep into the lives of characters that acquire human status through authors' masterful ability to journey into unknown territories . . . Still, when we read great works, we cannot stay outside. The reader is drawn into the plot, empathizes with some characters, hates others, mentally argues with or supports the writer's views and, most importantly, establishes connections between content, character behavior, and her own past or present circumstances. In other words, fruitful reading entails a reflexive attitude on the part of the reader.

Active reading, the only way to really profit from

---

* Dauzot J. A. and Dauzot S. M. *READING: The Teacher and the Learner.* John Wiley & Sons, Inc., New York, 1981.

books, is reflected in notes pencilled on the margins, highlighted phrases or passages, question and exclamation marks, crosses, and the like. Nothing can be more wrong than to think that a book is a "valuable," a "sacred" object that must be preserved intact. Books call for intervention, in the same way as some forms of contemporary visual art appropriate an object and make a new imprint on it, thus turning it into a unique object, for every intervention is exclusive and individual. The key, indeed, is appropriation. *Your* copy, *your* interaction with the story, *your* conclusions. Books have an ending, but are not truly finished until readers reinterpret and actualize them.

There are books and books, so how do we know which are great works? Well, there is no way of telling if the book is relatively recent, because the measure of a great work is time. Books that were written centuries ago and are still read have accomplished their destiny of evergreens for the simple reason that the issues they discuss are so profoundly human that we feel they inform the present. Your present, what may puzzle you about it, is explained and discussed in great works. Thus, you can learn much from books, not only about places you will never visit or people you will never meet, but about yourself for, in some way, those places and people duplicate your reality.

You might argue that the offer is so overwhelming

that, feeling at a loss to choose, you opt to spend your time otherwise engaged. You are right about the first part and wrong about the second. It is true that the "book population" in every possible format, including electronic and audio proposals, is growing exponentially. Still, reading is not a way of spending time but of *using* time profitably. You are a practical person. What could be more practical than to expand your knowledge without attending a regular, scheduled course? Can you possibly imagine the cost of private tuition with a great writer, at your own place, assuming the writer is alive and willing to humor you?

I would like to tell you about my own experience in regard to reading. To begin with, I was born in a home where you kept tripping over books. My parents never let a day go by without reading me a story, and at age four I grew impatient to begin reading by myself, so they indulged me by teaching me the skill rather early for the customs of the time. From then on, I never stopped. First as a child and then as a young teenager, I randomly devoured books without rhyme or reason. My mother would warn me against reading this or that book because it lay beyond my comprehension. Needless to say, the minute she left home I made for the "forbidden" book. Although later, more mature rereadings proved her right, I felt that I "understood." And I did, at the surface, more primary layer of the material. In other words, the exercise of reading never left me empty handed.

My studies in literature organized my approach to books, but that does not mean that you need special training to read. Leave that to specialists; you only need to open up to the book of your choice.

I began to write very young, published intermittently for many years, and have been making up for lost time since 2005. On the basis of my readings and my writing, I have selected a number of books that will no doubt grip you. In the coming chapters you will find information about them. You will realize that there are several layers of comprehension depending on how far you wish to go. You may be happy with what you apprehend on the surface or read further to enhance your knowledge of matters that the text hints at but does not explain. One book leads on to many. The decision, as always, lies with you.

Ideally, you should get a copy of the book discussed (or consider reading it after going over the corresponding chapter in this volume), a pen or pencil, the paragraph at the end of each section and, if you wish, a notebook to produce your own "book about the books."

Enjoy the journey you are about to start.

Reading for Personal Development

Fyodor Dostoevsky

Crime and Punishment

Roughly speaking, one could say that there are two kinds of fiction writers. Some stand aside, observe the world around them and then construct their stories by knitting connections between their observations (what is) and their imagination (what could be.) The others draw on their personal life, fictionalize private events to suit the genre chosen, and come up with great, most enlightening stories.

Fyodor Dostoevsky's experience as a political prisoner in Siberia in the mid-19th century, a consequence of his protests against the social dissolution Russia was undergoing, prompted him to write *Crime and Punishment* in the year of his liberation. Although it brushes on his experience, this novel conveys his thoughts about the very reasons why he had been sent into exile-prison: the country's falling apart through oppression, poverty, and corruption.

It is interesting to know that the first manuscript was written in the form of the main character's personal diary, and that from *Raskolnikov's Diary* there emerged the formidable work that was later published under the name we now know it. Dostoevsky is a blend of the two types of writers mentioned above. A real life episode that appeared in the press provided him with the incident that triggered the chain of suffering he so well narrated. On the other hand, his acute feelings about his country's decay provided the ancillary stories and reflections that intertwined with the main character's fate.

The story offers a detailed account of the agony that tortures the mind of a young, penniless student who has planned to commit a murder. Rodion Romanovich Raskolnikov has come to St. Petersburg to attend university, but his scanty means force him (or so he says) to give up his studies. He lives in a boarding house, cannot pay the rent, and feeds on the leftovers brought to him by a kind-hearted servant, for he cannot afford to pay for his food either. He pawns his painfully few valuables to Alyona Ivanovna, and the more he sees of her the more he hates her. In his mind, which has entered a confusional state partly because of his weak physical condition and partly because of bits and pieces of misunderstood philosophy, Ivanovna does not deserve to live. She is a leech, thriving on the despair of her patrons, and it would be a good and honorable deed to rid the world of this monster, steal her hoard, and use it for his own advancement in life. Raskolnikov thinks of himself as an "extraordinary man." Although Nietszche is never mentioned in the text, the theory of the Superman clearly pervades the argument. As an "extraordinary man," the protagonist is above the law, even more so when the money he is planning to "take" will enable him to graduate and thus help the society in which he lives.

An additional item to bear in mind is that the youngster's last name derives from a Russian word that means "schismatic" or "divided," and that this bears on our comprehension of his nature. In fact, Raskolnikov is torn both between the imagined steps implied in committing the crime and the factualness of actually killing, and seems to suffer from schizophrenia (a split or "divided" mind), and from some kind of manic depression. His mental condition sometimes drives him to feel that he will meet with success and others makes him sick with fear for the consequences of his recklessness.

Once he has hushed the internal voices that stay his hand, he finally murders Ivanovna in the clumsiest way possible, for the planning and the execution (the fantasy and the reality) prove to be irreconcilable. The sudden appearance of Ivanovna's sister when he is still trying to find cash in the apartment stains his conscience with another, unnecessary death.

From then on, the long way to redemption through punishment twists and turns into the recesses of the lives and circumstances of other characters who interact with Raskolnikov. Three of these protagonize stories within the story.

Marmeladov, a former public servant whose alcoholism leads his family into abject poverty and despair, embodies the thousands, perhaps millions of people who sank into unimaginable dejection amid the chaos that engulfed a once possible social order. In fact, Dostoevsky originally thought of making the curse of drinking the main theme of the novel, before realizing that drinking was not the disease but the symptom that things were very wrong.

Svidrigailov is a wealthy country squire ruled by his passions. Good and evil mean nothing to him, and even his passions sound shallow, as if triggered by a splenetic view of life rather than by genuine desire. His seemingly innate corruption makes his "acts of kindness" either sinister or meaningless, depending on the case.

Finally, Marmeladov's daughter Sonia, who loves and is loved by Raskolnikov, engineers one last and lasting transformation in Raskolnikov's healing process.

The women in the novel provide an extraordinary sampler of the feminine character. From the harpy to the near-saint, they succeed in living their lives as well as influencing the lives of the men they relate to. Then, as now, a man consciously or unconsciously depends on his view of women and on his fantasies about what the women around him think of *him*.

You may wonder what good will come to you from reading this novel. To begin with, although the characters live in a very distant past, the skill of the writer masterfully depicts human nature and the private outcomes of an unfair social order. Basically, man has not changed. Technological wonders lull us into believing that we have overcome our instincts; we sincerely tend to believe that we are more rational and civilized than were our predecessors. If you just look around you and, most importantly, if you look inside you, you are bound to admit that there is not much truth in such belief. *Crime and Punishment* is a comprehensive depiction of emotions, behaviors, philosophical revolutions, and relationships. Moreover, it shows a profound, non-judgmental understanding of man's dilemmas in an environment that he thinks he has conquered but whose laws he cannot escape.

It would be ideal if you could read the novel before going on to the next paragraph which, among other things, includes a comment on the ending.

The title of the novel suggests that it is structurally divided into two parts. However, as you must have realized by now, the idea of punishment is present long before the crime is committed. It takes the form of intense suffering, and is self-inflicted. The alleged right to commit a crime, fuelled by references to Napoleon and his ruthlessness for the sake of "the greater good," dwindles in the face of the fears that overcome Raskolnikov when he has already killed the two women. He discovers that he is not "an extraordinary man," but an ordinary one, to the point of extreme fragility. His dreams and bouts of fever punish him as he waits for ordinary justice to track him down and bring him to justice. It strikes us that we do not hear a word of regret for what he has done. With the unwavering love of Sonia filling his hours in prison, he finds peace in doing time in accordance with the court's ruling. Raskolnikov's epiphany, in a very loose sense of the word, is not synonymous with atonement. He does not seek redemption in a religious sense; his "salvation" depends entirely on his acceptance that he is no more and no less than a man and that, as a man, he is entitled to pay for his crime and move on.

You may have wondered why Raskolnikov turned himself in. Perhaps you have read Edgar Alan Poe's *The Tell-Tale Heart*. The similarities between the murderers in the two stories are worth pondering. In *Crime and*

Punishment, even if religion is carefully kept out of the picture, the perpetrator felt that confession would relieve his torment. On the other hand, Petrovich's sadistic "I—know—that—you—know—that—I—know" maneuvers slyly and cruelly exact total surrender. The invisible strings that connect Raskolnikov, Svidrigailov, and Petrovich knot tightly to bring about Raskolnikov's downfall. He that was metaphorically dies to allow the emergence of he that will be.

For further insight into this novel, it would be great if you could find information about the following:

Nihilism: wikipedia/ http://www.iep.utm.edu/nihilism
Friedrich Nietszche's Superman Theory: http://personal.ecu.edu/maccartyr/great/projects/Knowles.htm
Georg Hegel: http://plato.stanford.edu/entries/hegel
Søren Kierkegaard: http://plato.stanford.edu/entries/kierkegaard
Russia: wikipedia (History)

Aldous Huxley

Brave New World

At writing workshops, intending writers are insistently warned of the importance of a title. It should sound attractive and give a general idea of the contents without disclosing too much. Many a book is discarded because of an unfortunate title, and many sell exceedingly well thanks to a clever choice that sometimes arouses false expectations. The gurus running these workshops do not often remind their students that titles may well be fragments of works written by others. As a reader, you do not really care how a particular title occurred to the writer, but you should know when it has been borrowed from someone else's work. Such decisions are not capricious, and if you miss the intertextual connections between title and source you will probably also miss much of the writer's purpose.

Most writers leave recognition of links between works to us readers. In his text, Huxley explicitly connects the title of his book to Miranda's speech*. Yet not all of us have engaged in the kind of in-depth reading that would allow us to make instant associations between lines from different books.

The phrase "Brave New World," then, was borrowed from Shakespeare's *The Tempest*. In the play as in the novel, a new world is envisaged, although the respective authors were clearly not thinking about the same outcome.

Huxley's book blends science fiction with negative utopia to reach a climax of dystopia†. Consider that in 1932, when the novel was first published, he anticipated scientific and technological advances that only came under experimentation much later: chemical contraception, cloning, a drug that sounds as a forerunner of LSD, and the *feelies*‡ among others. The inclusion of such devices intended to contribute to perfect bliss in a flawless society.

Unlike a number of fictional works, mostly cinematic, in which a devastating war leaves a bunch of survivors in the primitive state of cavemen, Huxley's novel retains survivors with their knowledge and skills intact. These characters wisely avoid making the mistakes that allegedly led to the war by developing

---

* *The Tempest*, Act V, Scene I.
† Negative utopia. Usually a futuristic society that has degraded into a repressive, controlled state (answers.com)
‡ Movies that provide the viewer with sensorial experiences.

science and technology and doing away with overpopulation, religious beliefs, political regimes, social paradigms, and psychoanalytical findings that (so they say) contributed to human misery in the imaginary past era.

Interestingly, the new order banned literature, on the grounds that it would be too dangerous to expose Alpha-Plus Intellectuals to the dangers of going beyond the boundaries of their caste. For one of the keys to the success of the new society lay in the fact that classes; i.e., social mobility, had been replaced by castes; i.e., zero chance of social mobility.

After the new society had been devised, the existing population was given the choice of a happy life in the new world under strict rules or an uncertain existence in a place called the Reservation, which resembled the previous conditions of existence. No crossing of boundaries was allowed, mostly to protect the new society from those who, having opted for freedom without the aid of science, were bound to suffer regression to primitive ways of life in which disease, superstition, and barbaric customs took a heavy toll on the descendants of the first self-exiled generation.

The attentive reader perceives that not everything that glitters is gold in the new world. The chinks in the would-be armor-clad organization confirm the divorce between man and perfection. Still, lapses could be kept in hand tolerably well until the Savage—a young inhabitant of the Reservation—found his way into the "civilized area" of the world.

Owing to the peculiar circumstances of his birth (which you will find out as you read the book), the Savage had learned to read. One day, at the age of twelve, he had come across a tattered volume of *The Complete Works of William Shakespeare*. With his mother's permission, he opened it and hit upon one of Hamlet's soliloquies.

> The strange words rolled through his mind; rumbled, like talking thunder; like the drums at the summer dances, if the drums could have spoken; like the men singing the Corn Song, beautiful, beautiful, so that you cried [...] because it talked to him, talked wonderfully, and only half-understandably, a terrible beautiful magic [...]

The Savage read and reread the plays until he knew them by heart. Every single line helped him make sense of the many things that baffled him, of the feelings that crept over him and filled his heart with anguish and longing. The time came when he interpreted the world literally—though not literarily—through Shakespeare's eyes.

With this baggage he crossed the border.

What follows reminds one very much of the notion of the outsider developed in Harold Pinter's plays of the Absurd. Stable systems do not admit of new elements unless they have the flexibility to change their fixed positions, thus making room for the newcomer to settle in. Just as in Pinter's plays the outsider disrupts the system, calling into question roles and identities that no one has doubted; so far, in *Brave New World* the Savage's presence and expectations pierce through the flimsy protective tissue that the elders have woven. The pace of the story quickens towards a cruel yet logically expectable ending to be read as a warning that tampering with human nature, even if done in good faith, may eventually lead to disaster.

Brief though this comment is, the issue of dehumanization involved in the pursuit of happiness cannot have escaped you. Huxley's unparalleled description of a world that is still very much our own will at least alert you to the perils of certain human achievements. In his prologue to the 1946 edition of the novel, Huxley states that "this is a book about the future." Well, the future is now. Therefore, this is a book about the present, but at the same time it offers a warning about a future yet to come unless we give some serious thought to the way in which we steer our lives.

It would be ideal if you could read the novel before going on to the next paragraph which, among other things, includes a comment on the ending.

The worst form of totalitarianism is that which disguises itself as something else. Suddenly, one "enlightened" character or a small group of such characters decide to play Father to a large population. The "enlightened" ones claim to know better, to know what the others actually need and desire. This is typical of perversion. The creepiest feature of the totalitarian regime depicted in *Brave New World* is that everything looks perfectly reasonable and kind.

The values that hold societies together—love, family, religion—have been dispensed with on the grounds that they undermine "COMMUNITY, IDENTITY, STABILITY." It does not require much imagination to recognize the "Liberty, Equality, Fraternity" motto of the French Revolution, and we have all learned by now how miserably these noble notions failed. In the view of the enlightened leaders of the new order, failure is always due to human factors; therefore, human factors must be suppressed, with neo-Pavlovian conditioning ensuring general happiness. And it works, to a point. The book is laden with name symbolism. The main characters bear names that have weighed heavily on past history, only the history that they are taught has been tailored to erase the significance of such names. Yet some of these characters unknowingly and hopelessly experience the urges that led their namesakes to major breakthroughs.

The arrival of John the Savage shakes the foundations of the new world. He should be read as a Christ figure archetype that, in doing penitence for his own misconceptions and for the flaws of the society into which he was transplanted, ends up by hanging himself. Thus Christ the sacrificial lamb and Judas the repentant traitor become two in one and leave us wondering about the consequences of our collective actions when we have renounced individuality for the sake of safety amid the flock.

For further insight into this novel, it would be great if you could read/find information about the following:

Huxley, Aldous: *Brave New World Revisited* (1958)
Malthusian catastrophe: en.wikipedia.org/wiki/
   Malthusian_catastrophe
Neo-Pavlovian conditioning: wikipedia
The Oedipus complex: http://www.bookrags.com/
   tandf/oedipus-complex-2-tf/
Shakespeare, William: *The Tempest*
Hermann von Helmholtz
John B. Watson
Henry Ford and the Assembly Line

Hermann Hesse

Steppenwolf

Steppenwolf confronts you with a structure of Chinese boxes*. The first narrator claims to have made the acquaintance of an outlandish character that lodged at his aunt's boarding house. The second narrator is Harry Haller, the lodger himself, who reproduces an anonymous opuscule he claims to have received in the street from a complete stranger. The gift bears the title *Treaties of the Steppenwolf. Not for everyone.* Once Harry and the reader have had the chance to go through it, Harry resumes the narration.

The *Treaties* compare man with the wolf of the steppes. In truth, man upholds two contradictory beliefs about his kind. On the one hand, owing to a deeply rooted Christian tradition, man is convinced that he

---

* A number of boxes of different sizes tightly fit inside one another. You can see the outermost one, but as you open it, you find another, which in turn reveals another, and so forth. Here, of course, the expression has been used metaphorically. In literature, the expression refers to a narrative contained inside another. This device can offer different perspectives of a story that, depending on how you consider it, is and is not the same.

is ruled by the duality good–evil. On the other hand, he entertains the illusion that his nature consists of an unfissured totality. The anonymous author contends that men who have foregone the latter belief attribute all the fine qualities of our nature to our human half (the principle of good) while stuffing our wolf persona* (the principle of evil) with unlikable, disgusting, or downright immoral aspects that disturb us. The analysis of such self-appeasing notion extends much farther, reaching a startling climax with the assertion that, in fact, man is inhabited by a myriad of mindsets that alternately displace one another. Unable or unwilling to cope with them, he hypocritically chooses to ignore what does not fit into the good–evil pair.

You start losing your foothold on reality when you realize that the character depicted as the paradigmatic wolf of the steppes in the opuscule is called Harry Haller. At this point, you have an inkling that not everything in the text belongs in the real world created by the narrative.

The Harry you first met through the landlady's nephew is weary of life and feels overcome by an inclination to a particularly bloody form of suicide. In the ambivalent mood that characterizes his discourse and behavior, he turns the idea around in his mind,

---

* In this case, an aspect of personality.

at once horrified and fascinated by the picture of his death. Like every other individual undergoing this predicament, he calms down when he has finally decided to make his exit. Paradoxically, he can now enjoy the precious little on which he sets some value. There is no need to rush into the fatal act, because he knows that what caused his anguish—to die or not to die by his own hand—has been satisfactorily taken care of. Please allow me a small digression here. Such is the case with all suicides that do not react thoughtlessly to a moment's despair. When you fear for them as you see them at their worst, they have not yet reached a conclusion. But when you observe a change of heart, a relaxed, even content disposition it is because they have stopped struggling against the temptation to let destiny decide for them. This is the time when you should really worry.

The man who had given Harry the *Treaties* carried, that very night, a banner announcing an Anarchist evening at a Magic Theater, but had refused to feed the details to Harry on the grounds that it was *not for everyone*. Anarchism, magic, or the fact of being excluded whetted his desire to find his way into the Theater. However, he was denied the chance of finding the way in. One day he recognized the stranger among the mourners attending a burial. Approaching him casually, Harry asked about the soirée that evening, but the man seemed to have no idea of what he meant, and directed him to *The Black Eagle* (some sort of night club), remarking that it might fulfill his expectations.

Harry felt that the time to die had come. He was at once terrified and persuaded of the inevitability of the end. Still, why not give himself Dutch courage and drink his cup to the dregs before the fatal act? So he made himself drunk at successive bars, and finally staggered into *The Black Eagle.* He sat by a beautiful, mysterious girl who seemed to know his most hidden thoughts, mothered him in his time of need, flirted with him, and predicted that from then on he would obey her orders because he desperately needed to be subdued, that he would eventually fall in love with her, and that in due course she would order him to do something unspeakable, and to that too he would agree, though with a heavy heart.

The girl would not tell Harry her name, so he called her Hermine—not a totally capricious choice, as you will discover later on. Hermine, then, slowly and steadily reconciled him to the bourgeois, superficial lifestyle that he so despised. And when the wolf of the steppes reluctantly yielded to the man of the world, Hermine and her chum Pablo, another shady and shadowy character, facilitated his access to the Magic Theater, where he was expected to obey her final order. Harry found it so unbearable that he refused even to consider it. But the stage had been set, and he could do nothing but face the challenge. His success or failure would show whether or not Harry had learned something from his mentor.

How much of this is real in terms of Harry's life may be inferred from a little speech by Pablo just before he shows Harry round the Theater.

> [. . .] You are looking for the world inhabited by your own soul. That other reality for which you yearn lives exclusively inside you. I cannot give you anything that lacks existence in your inner self. The only picture gallery that I can show you is the one in your soul. I can only provide you with the occasion, the drive, and the key. I will help to render your own world visible. That is all.*

In Harry's dreams and thoughts, his interlocutors are Goethe and Mozart, with Wagner, Haydn, and Brahms passing fleetingly by. His unquenchable suffering stems from the fact that he is only too well aware of man's lack of harmony with himself and the world, and that he does not settle for what practically everyone else would regard as "a normal life." You will

---

* My translation.

find many more Chinese boxes inside this extraordinary novel, so do not imagine for a moment that you already know the story.

It would be ideal if you could read the novel before going on to the next paragraph which, among other things, includes a comment on the ending.

It is said that Hermann Hesse complained that this particular work had been grossly misunderstood. The time had not yet come when we agreed that, regardless of the writer's purpose, different readers could interpret a literary work in different ways as long as the proposed interpretations were justified from the text. You must have noticed that *Steppenwolf* develops a number of parallel themes, that it may be understood as an object lesson in philosophy, and that the notion of the quest, present in many other major works, stands out from the very beginning, as could be expected from a writer who stepped out of the expectations placed on him by his family to pursue some essential truth in alien religions and disciplines.

The difficulty to distinguish between fantasy and reality in the life of Harry Haller may be crucial to understanding his crime. In fact, if the Magic Theater is no more than a game of mirrors populated by composite fragments of his past and projected images of the protective figures in charge of his rehabilitation, he has killed nobody even if the knife itself was real. However, because in this story intentions count more than actions, it does not really matter that the murder was fictitious: what counts is that a real knife conveys the determination of stabbing a real creature. Pablo's final rebuke precisely addresses this issue: in spite of all his efforts, Harry has not learned to play the game of life.

You should not let the emphasis on Harry's existential anguish distract you from the possibility of salvation here and now. After all, the only thing he needs do is restart the game from scratch. Nietzsche's theory of eternal recurrence reminds you that the game can be played forever or, in this case, until the kernel lesson has been thoroughly learned.

For further insight into this novel, it would be great if you could find information about/read the following:

Nietszche, Friedrich: *Thus Spake Zarathustra*
Goethe, Johann W. Von: *Faust*
Hesse, Hermann: *Siddartha*
Stendhal: *The Life of Mozart*
Brill, A. A.: *Basic Principles of Psychoanalysis*,
   http://www.institutobios.org/catharsis.pdf

Juan Rulfo

Pedro Páramo

Pedro Páramo belongs in the recently devalued and looked-down-on realm of magic realism. In literature as in most of the things that make up our daily routine, fashion dictates what is in and what is out. If you read only because your social/work environment demands that you do so, you will miss much of what is valuable once the season is over.

Broadly speaking, magic realism embraces all works in which the fantastic or impossible blends with the real in what seems a perfectly reasonable continuum. In other words, the magic aspects of the narrative are presented as if they were completely natural and true to life within the boundaries set by the story. To Western readers unfamiliar with myth and ancient religions, such books prove, at most, poetic and entertaining. Still, what you should bear in mind when tackling any of these works is that they offer you the opportunity to exercise your brain to the limit. The reason for this is that the temporal and spatial elements that usually guide the reader in conventional fiction have been conveniently blurred, as have the identities of the multiple voices* that compose the narration. Thus each voice tells basically the same story but, since the point of view shifts, the endlessly repeated story is nuanced every time with new details and perspectives. The uncanny aspects of this type of literature challenge the reader to find the links that hold together worlds, archetypal characters, and views of life that stand miles and eons apart in the composition of the text. You may take up the challenge and include yourself into what cannot be explained by logic, or dismiss it as a pastime. In either case you will be richer for the experience, though if you opt for the first proposal you may reach the startling conclusion that in real life, your own life, I mean, plenty of events seem to mock attempts at logical explanations. Hamlet's phrase "There are more things in heaven and earth, Horatio/ Than are dreamt of in your philosophy"† already anticipated the multiplicity of meanings that the magic realists laid bare in the 20th century. Giving the word "philosophy" a generous scope will permit you to connect ancient beliefs in another, more superstitious and fearful kind of magic with the unexplainable in modern man's heart and anxiety.

---

* A character's distinctive manner of expression.
† *Hamlet,* Act I, Scene V.

Because of the very nature of the genre, one does not really detect a straightforward plot in *Pedro Páramo*. Very simply put, the novel begins with a young man who has just lost his mother and has arrived at a one-horse Mexican village to make the acquaintance of Pedro Páramo, the father he never met because his mother fled the place before giving birth.

This story branches out into many others, including the life and times of Pedro Páramo himself against the background of the early 20th century civil wars that devastated the country. You learn about brutal men who duplicate a merciless landscape, of women at the mercy of the men and of their own unbridled passions, of a priest who fights cupidity but cannot help dishonoring his vows, of murder, bribery, treason, insanity, and infinite loneliness.

Once more the theme of the quest reemerges. Each of the characters pursues, in a way, the meaning of life in general and of his/her own fate in particular. At times, their voices mingle in one single narrative; on other occasions one voice stands out from the rest to furnish you with details that shed light on specific aspects of the intertwined stories.

Pedro Páramo, long dead at the beginning of the novel, is the fixed star around which the men and women in the village revolve like planets in a solar system. A dark, threatening, fearful star, but the one that holds together the mini-cosmos called Comala.

Although the place actually exists and is known as one of Mexico's *pueblos mágicos* (magic towns), I would venture to say that it was chosen because it suggests a condensation of *cosa mala* (a bad thing). In fact, nothing good ever happened in Comala; it seems as if every evil has set up camp in the lands and the souls of its inhabitants.

The novel is by no means judgmental. With far-sighted deliberation, Rulfo leaves you alone with the twists and turns of the lives he depicts. Not that he expects you to judge either; I rather believe that he hopes that you will understand and commiserate, or commiserate even when you do not understand.

The most striking feature of this masterpiece is the lack of barriers between the living and the dead. In other words, the dead are not aware that they are sleeping in graves as their shadows mechanically perform the routinary movements of what used to be their uneventful or tragic lives, depending on the case, and the living do not seem to make the difference between their state and that of their departed.

In the altered timeline of the narrative, the past with its balance of life and death and the present in which life is a lingering memory that finally fades to disintegration in dust coexist without bothering each other. One is reminded of "death's other Kingdom,"* Eliot's brilliant reminder that the world of the living may well be death's one kingdom.

When Juan Preciado, the son in search of his father, arrives at Comala, he is warned that Pedro Páramo has passed away, like everyone else on the *Media Luna* estate that was his abode. Still, he is not warned that *all* the villagers are dead, including his occasional guide and informer. Moreover, Juan Preciado cannot outlive his own terrors, so very soon in the story he joins the ghostly hosts that haunt the town.

That the dead mimic the living is not an original idea. It goes at least as far back as the ancient Greeks. What is new and thought-provoking is that these dead seem to believe that nothing has changed during their passage and that no noticeable differences can be established between them in the afterlife and them in the hinterlife.† The resulting monotone might point to the fact that, at least in terms of magic realism, no such passage takes place, and that the living and the dead breathe the same air, share the same spaces, and enjoy each other's company at will. Incidentally, the dead get the best of both worlds, for they can choose to roam the streets and make themselves at home in abandoned houses (sometimes perhaps their own) or

---

* T. S. Eliot, *The Hollow Men*, 1925.
† My term for actual life in the world.

lie in their graves, whereas the living are denied the comforts of the cemetery.

Besides the intriguing elements put in play by this amazing author, one cannot but wonder whether the downplay of the dead–alive theme does not connote a remark about *us*. How alive are we? Or, if you will, to what extent does the daily repetition of acts that have long lost their meaning ensure that we still rank among the living? Stretching it one inch further, perhaps this sample of magic realism metaphorizes a profoundly disturbing question about life itself, with no magic attached to it.

It would be ideal if you could read the novel before going on to the next paragraph which, among other things, includes a comment on the ending.

It is said that places and people live, figuratively speaking, as long as someone remembers them. If we were not dealing with magic realism, the village described in the novel would have been erased from human memory insofar as no one survived to recall its history and no records were kept of its existence. However, especially among those whom we proud, skeptical city dwellers call "primitive" people, there are ultrasensitive souls unspoiled by modernization and technology. Such souls claim to have the gift of sensing certain presences and of communicating with them. We tend to call the presences "ghosts" and the phenomenon "deceit."

I am not making a case for the possibility of bridging two worlds, mostly because I am not even convinced that there is a world other than this. My point is that lack of knowledge/evidence/data does not necessarily mean that things we know little or nothing about do not exist. If the opposite line of reasoning were true, we would all be Schrödinger's cat* (half-dead and half-alive), for indeed we do not exist to those who know nothing about us.

Then, perhaps these presences deserve to be taken seriously, though not in the guise magic realism shows them. You may have felt encouraged to undertake a certain course of action or discouraged from doing so by a memory of a beloved dead, or experienced an exchange with her in your dreams, for example. It is up to you to decide whether your mind is playing tricks on you or whether two planes of existence can and do cross paths.

Because of the blurred temporal edges of this kind of literature, the ending of *Pedro Páramo*, with Pedro dying in the arms of an already dead servant who

---

* See *Schrödinger's cat* at Wikipedia.

discharged her duties all the same, could have been the beginning. This serves as a reminder that, unlike other novels of the genre, *Pedro Páramo* offers a special bonus: you can begin reading wherever you like for, regardless of your chosen starting point, the story will complete itself in the only possible way.

No further reading will enhance your insight into this novel. However, you might like to read others of the same kind.

García Márquez, Gabriel: *One Hundred Years of Solitude*
Rushdie, Salman: *The Satanic Verses*
Allende, Isabel: *The House of the Spirits*
Esquivel, Laura: *Like Water for Chocolate*

Sándor Márai

Embers

A retired General has lived in self-imposed confinement for forty years. His home is a stunning castle built by his ancestors in the Hungarian woods, but he has renounced the spacious, majestic rooms and halls with their luxurious furniture, artworks, and mementos for the safety of the dark old wing where he was born and where he expects to die.

One day he, whose affairs are managed by administrators and gamekeepers; he, who entertains neighbors and dignitaries by proxy, leaving everything in the able hands of his stewards, agrees to receive a guest for dinner.

The General has expected this moment for forty-one years and forty-three days.

One spends a lifetime preparing for something. First one suffers the wound. Then one plans revenge. And waits.

As the hours drag on, the General reminisces on the past. He first met Konrad, the man he will soon see one last time, at the military academy in Vienna where both were new cadets. Following the "opposites attract" theory, Henrik the aristocrat and Konrad the only child of a poor family became best friends. It would seem as if an invisible thread kept them together through thick and thin, for they had an altogether different view of beauty, duty, love, leisure, pleasure. . . . The general has had all the time in the world to dissect their relationship:

> [. . .] because of their friendship, each forgave the other's original sin: wealth on the one hand and poverty on the other.

In the eve of his life, the General is no longer sure about practically anything.

"[. . .] a complicated and enigmatic relationship commonly covered by the word 'friendship,'" he reflects, but he does unhesitatingly believe that all that matters is the truth, that "facts are not the truth," and that "it is precisely the words one utters, or stifles, or writes, that are the issue, if not the only issue."

The only reason, then, why he will open his doors to Konrad after some forty years of silence on both parts is that he needs to find out the truth before he surrenders his worn body to the earth. What truth?

The crevices of his mind release bits and pieces of events past but not forgotten, like the occasions when Konrad and the General's mother made music together. Henrik neither liked nor understood classical music. He regarded it as "forces that shake and explode structures of order which man has devised to conceal what lies beneath." Konrad, who claimed kinship to Chopin on his mother's side, felt that "the melodies did not speak to the rational portion of his mind," so one could say that the very same features of music that aroused Henrik's discomfort awoke Konrad's most sublime emotions. The General also recalled that Konrad, whose meager income prevented him even from feeding properly, had never accepted a penny from him. "Whoever refuses to accept a part wants the whole, wants everything." Yet such thoughts did not come to him in his youth. We attain wisdom, if ever, when it is too late to mend our ways.

In due course, Henrik married Krisztina, the daughter of a man who copied scores for Konrad. He fell so much in love with her that he did not mind at all the class difference between them. You can laugh it off now, but it was a serious hindrance in the rigid social stratification that melted away in the rivers of blood let loose during World War I. Krisztina honored her husband and her duties as an aristocrat's wife. Moreover, she naturally occupied her place as a third party in the by then long-standing comradeship between Henrik and Konrad.

It all went smoothly until what the General called "the day of the hunt." On the evening of that day, the three of them dined together as usual. And the next morning, Konrad disappeared from their lives, from his lodgings in the city, from the face of the earth.

You could then assume that the truth that the General sought was an answer as to why his friend had behaved in a manner that amounted to betrayal. And if you did, you would be wrong.

This extraordinary novel is somehow divided into two parts. The first focuses on the old General nesting in what used to be his mother's rooms, going over his childhood and youth memories and feelings as he instructs his most trusted servant to set the table in exactly the same room and way in which it was set on the evening when Konrad last had dinner in the castle and to serve exactly the same courses in the same order. The second consists of the conversation between host and guest during and after dinner. Perhaps the word "conversation" does not aptly describe what passed between the two men. Although the General addressed Konrad, you feel that most of the time he was talking to himself or, rather, arguing a case with himself. Konrad listened without interrupting, answered sparsely when asked a direct question, and volunteered some information about his whereabouts following the night of his disappearance.

What he disclosed about his life confirmed that "he would never be a soldier," an enigmatic dictum uttered by Henrik's father when he first met Konrad as a child. The fact that Konrad graduated from the academy and took up his commission in the army seemed to belie the Officer of the Guards' judgement of character. Only much later did Henrik understand what his father had meant by "soldier."

Both men knew that this reunion was as necessary as it was final. Gaping wounds needed stitching. One last view of what each of them had been to the other in the light of what they were now might set their minds at rest. They were too near the end of the downward slope to rekindle grudges. All they wanted was to find forgiveness without atonement, for each man in his own, particular way, swayed between a sense of guilt and a sense of inevitability.

One wonders if either gentleman found some relief in the accusations and confessions suavely made that evening. Perhaps. Yet one of the most appealing traits in this novel is that Márai not once appealed to remorse or repentance to smooth the blunt edges of his characters.

It would be ideal if you could read the novel before

going on to the next paragraph which, among other things, includes a comment on the ending.

The shadows of the dead lurk around the corners of the castle. These dead are brought back to life in the vivid memories of the General and his former friend but, most importantly, Krisztina plays a protagonic role even from her grave. One cannot but wonder what drove these three people to betray their own feelings. Among the many possible explanations, the novel contains a revealing sentence that might well prove more satisfactory than conventional or parochial attempts at an answer:

> Every exercise of power incorporates a faint, almost imperceptible element of contempt for those over whom the power is exercised.

If you look carefully into the three main characters, you will notice that each of them exercised some kind of power on the other two, and that they all lost their peace of mind as a consequence of the giddying circle of power that stopped abruptly when Konrad broke loose from its fascination.

Among other things, the General lays emphasis on

the fact that "it is part of our human condition to kill." He is referring to the moment when he thought that Konrad would shoot him dead during the hunt, but he also felt partly responsible for his wife's death insofar as he "killed" her in his mind as soon as he realized what was transpiring between her and Konrad. That humans cannot avoid killing and, more precisely, killing someone they love, had already been pinpointed in Oscar Wilde's *The Ballad of Reading Gaol*, published nearly half a century before Márai composed his story.* On the other hand, the life drive as described by Freud pulled Konrad away from murder but plunged him into spiritual death. He buried himself in the tropics, and "the tropics are a disease." Drawing on *The Fall of Edward Barnard*[†], what one would loosely call "the tropics" can be a cure to the hypocritical ways of society, regardless of the extent to which social conventions have changed. For the whole point, you see, is that they have changed but not vanished, and we are still prey to the ones that shape our times.

---

* "Yet each man kills the thing he loves
By each let this be heard.
Some do it with a bitter look,
Some with a flattering word.
The coward does it with a kiss,
The brave man with a sword!"
Fragment of *The Ballad of Reading Gaol*.
† A short story by Somerset Maugham, first published in 1921.

Then, if you are ailing as was Konrad, your diseased soul will walk beside you wherever you go.

At the end of the story, with the dead back in their tombs and the partly living ready to depart, nothing matters any more. Krisztina remains lost to both her lovers, her portrait is restored to its place, for it has lost the power to hurt, and one last crime—a crime of pity, if you wish—has fleetingly restored the old complicity between Henrik and Konrad when they burn to cinders Krisztina's diary and its well-hidden secrets.

For further insight into this novel, it would be great if you could find information about/read the following:

The Austro-Hungarian Empire:
    http://www.beyondbooks.com/eur12/2d.asp
Conrad, Joseph: *The Heart of Darkness*
Maugham, Somerset: *The Fall of Edward Barnard*
Rilke, Rainer Maria: *Letters to a Young Poet*
Wilde, Oscar: *The Ballad of Reading Gaol*

Miguel Ángel Asturias

The President

I do not think that one can fully comprehend the nature of evil unless one has, so to speak, bled over this novel. Asturias develops a story that will sound quite familiar to Latin American readers, for every single one of our countries has suffered one or more cruel dictatorships, disturbingly weird to inhabitants of well-established democracies.

In real life, most Latin American dictatorial governments resulted from a military coup that ousted an elected civilian President. To a greater or lesser degree, such governments were guilty of corruption, political imprisonment, torture, and murder. What kept them one inch away from total evil was that, in their folly, the usurpers sometimes believed that their crimes served the greater good of the country. In a few cases, when cynicism dictated patriotic discourses while the usurpers in power harbored no doubts that the only greater good they had in mind was draining the country's resources, at least they moved as a class, or a clan, or a society within society. In other words, the members of the class were safe, even if no one else was.

The President deploys a collection of unspeakable abominations. Unspeakable, but Asturias found a voice to harmonize them and, what is even creepier, he put together this sampler of horrors in what we call "poetic prose." For the language is indeed rich and stunningly beautiful, so the stark contrast between the words and the events emphasizes the unbounded brutality of the narrative. As you read, you cannot but repeat to yourself that "this is a novel, and although these events surely happened somewhere, they did not all happen at the same time in the same place." Yet the disturbing thought that perhaps they did haunts you to the very end, given that the story is indeed convincing and the author was ruthlessly persecuted on account of this particular book.

The system of power depicted in the novel is cannibalistic. From the President down, every character, regardless of social status or political affiliation, preys on someone else. The vivid image of the buzzards constantly hovering above city and wilderness alike aptly metaphorizes the notion that, sooner or later, those in high places and those who have no place will eventually become carrion.

The President feels that life owes him. Unable to overcome the humiliations that he and his mother underwent when he was a ragged urchin, he made his way into politics, schemed, betrayed, filled people's ears with the lies he knew they thirsted for, and firmly installed himself at the head of a well-oiled regime in which perpetual reelection—for he was now a constitutional president, mind you—was his main purpose. A lifetime of revenge on those who maltreated him would be barely enough. Never mind that a majority of his victims had not been born in his nightmarish childhood. Never mind that many of the men and women who agonized in his dungeons could have been his fellow-sufferers. (Any similarities with contemporary history are purely coincidental. After all, this book was begun in Guatemala in 1922 and completed in Paris in 1932.)

All traitors, conspirators, and murderers fear getting a taste of the same medicine they so freely administer. The President, then, saw cloaks and daggers everywhere around him, and the asskissers who played informers to his paranoia fed him tales about people they themselves wanted destroyed out of spite, hatred, envy, or just because.

Thus the ring of evil was set in motion for, in due course, the informers were accused too and punished accordingly.

At the beginning of the narrative you are launched into the destitute that take shelter for the night at the entrance to the Cathedral. These creatures remind you of the Court of Miracles*, only the ones in *The President* are genuine, not dissemblers like most of the inhabitants of the Parisian underworld. A high-rank military happens to pass by and insult a crazy beggar who supposedly blocks his way. The beggar kills him and flees into the dark.

The President's eyes and ears soon learn what has really happened, but the crime proves a real godsend to incriminate a General and an intellectual believed to be plotting against the President. The beggars who witnessed the scene were rallied round, interrogated, and prompted to give the "right" answer. After a couple of them were savagely tortured for insisting on what they had seen—the truth—the others chose to name the two characters that the President wanted arrested on "legitimate" grounds. Not that this saved the lives of the actual killer or of the bunch of poor souls that used to crawl beside the Cathedral every night. In this particular rule of law, the only reliable witness was one who would be permanently deprived of the light of day. If he/she was too weak to survive imprisonment pending trial (to be held on an unnamed day of an unnamed year), too bad. The system was in no way to blame.

---

* In Victor Hugo's *The Hunchback of Notre Dame*, but also mentioned by other French authors such as François Villon and Alexandre Dumas.

Amid the stink of ministers doing business with madams and privileged professionals plundering the estates of lukewarm followers or illiterate *bona fide* peasants who never dallied with politics, one of the President's most trusted and lethal servants made a terrible mistake. Angel Face, for such was his nickname, frequently followed by the remark that his beauty paralleled Satan's, felt sorry for the wrong woman. And then he fell in love with her. And then he married her, and passed into the true realm of Satan, whose favorite son he was. (Was he not the President's pet?) In his imagination, he was alternately torn to pieces by wild dogs and forgiven with a benevolent smile; in real life, fear of his master's revenge clutched his heart, but confidence in his usefulness and knowledge of so many terrible secrets eased his mind. He would conquer where others had succumbed. He was a changed man who distributed life-saving information with the same generosity as he had singled people out for death.

The President rebuked him slightly for not having married in style and perfectly understood that love is blind. The Father of the People, the Hope of Democracy, the Defender of the Weak (!!!), for we never learn the President's real name, was able to tell loyalty from abject servitude. He forgot and forgave. Or so Angel Face chose to believe.

It would be ideal if you could read the novel before

going on to the next paragraph which, among other things, includes a comment on the ending.

Many characters in this novel experience intriguing dreams. Although in some cases the content and/or the form of the dreams might be explained by the rich symbols of the ancient Maya religion, one cannot but agree that life under a dictatorship seems to have a dreamlike quality. At times the dream envelops reality in welcome physical and spiritual comfort; on other occasions events draw nightmarish patterns. The assertion that the world of dreams overpowers the characters is based on the fact that no one feels ready to look at the surrounding horror straight in the face.

Just examine the attitudes of the different groups depicted by Asturias. The destitute know exactly what is going on in every corner of the city. However, they are too busy trying to survive one more hour if not one more day. Their survival depends on passing unnoticed rather than on food, alms, and tricks played on members of other classes. Unfortunately, the accidental murder of the President's favorite at their refuge drags them into what they so carefully meant to avoid. Their individual destinies fall upon them as something they will not comprehend, for they die cruel deaths because they will not lie.

This is one of the points when one might introduce the mythic theme, since the Mayans believed, for example, that men had been set on the Earth in order to feed the gods with their blood, flesh, and bones.

The middle and upper middle class, in no way ignorant of what kind of government has taken over the country, praise the President's rule for the very same reason: they do not want to have their property confiscated or be dragged to the fearful dungeons where the opponents rot, or shot in their own homes for opening their mouths against atrocity. They thus pretend that everything is fine, and live in fear that a wrong word or a wrong gesture may toss them over the protective fence they have built around themselves. These people have managed to entangle dream and reality to such an extent that they can no longer tell one from the other.

Angel Face's redemption through love seems to remind us that no good deed goes unpunished. He and his wife also march in the spectral parade toward death that opens and closes the story. In all likelihood, you have no direct experience of a political regime such as this. All the more reason to peek into it. Reading *The President* will set you wondering about some well-known political, social, and economic leaders, and render the invisible (the poor wretches that fall off every democratic system these days) visible to your eyes.

For further insight into this novel, it would be great if you could find information about/read the following:

Eliade, Mircea: *The Serpent*
Miller, Mary Ellen & Taube, Karl: *An Illustrated Dictionary of the Gods and Symbols of Ancient Mexico and the Maya*
Orwell, George: *1984*
Manuel José Estrada Cabrera: worldlingo.com/ma/enwiki/en/Manuel_Estrada_Cabrera

Giuseppe Tomasi di Lampedusa

The Leopard

The history of this book is at least as interesting as the novel itself. Information scattered here and there warns you that *The Leopard* was rejected by a couple of important Italian publishing houses during the author's lifetime. However, Giorgio Bassani, a great novelist and editor in his own right who wrote the prologue to the 1958 Feltrinelli* publication, distinctly tells us that Lampedusa had hardly finished copying the novel when he was overtaken by the illness that led to his death a couple of weeks later.

Bassani's narrative of the way in which he came by *The Leopard* raises a question about whether Lampedusa actually intended to have his work published. This much can be said: he was content to have finally put pen to paper in order to materialize a historical novel that he had been maturing for twenty-five years. The manuscript was sent—we do not know

---

* Giangiacomo Feltrinelli, Editore, Milano, Italy.

by whom—to a friend in Sicily, Lampedusa's own fatherland, and this friend passed it on to a Neapolitan lady living in Rome. She kept it until she heard that Bassani was involved in the release of a collection of novels, and mailed it to him, remarking that she thought it worth considering and that there was no name attached to the work. After reading the book, Bassani decided that it was a masterpiece. The very content led him to make inquiries in Palermo, where it became clear who the author was. In this rather erratic way a book that might have remained forever hidden from the public found its way to libraries and bookcases all over the world.

A contemporary Spanish critic has declared that, when writers do not destroy their unpublished/unfinished works before dying, they will sooner or later end up published, which is not always a good thing. But if caring hands had not preserved *The Leopard* until Bassani recognized it for the great work it is, we would have missed a sharp political view that, in many countries, still shows the measure of a particular kind of compromise.

In more than one way, rather than a historical novel, Lampedusa chronicled a family's history against the backdrop of the changes that led to the unification of Italy under the House of Savoy in 1861.

Fabrizio Corbera, Prince of Salina, resided with his

family in Palermo, Sicily. He ambivalently entertained the idea that he was an *alter ego* of the leopard on the Salina's coat of arms while realizing that hard times lay ahead, particularly for the old aristocracy to which he belonged. Giuseppe Garibaldi* had already begun his military campaign to turn Italy into a parliamentary monarchy, and it was not clear to many whether his partisans might, at some point, overthrow the established order and impose the liberal, republican ideas that their leader had embraced in earlier years. The Prince of Salina was, besides, troubled and annoyed that Tancredi Falconeri, his favorite nephew whom he had raised as his own son after the boy tragically lost both his parents, had decided to join Garibaldi's (irregular) army.

Very early in the story, the parting dialogue between uncle and nephew sets down the main theme, the one that has survived throughout generations and will, no doubt, endure till the end of times. Tancredi explains to Fabrizio that if they (the aristocrats) are not there, the republicans will prevail. "If we want things to stay as they are, things will have to change." Nowadays we call these strategies "cosmetic changes." The fact remains that the aristocrats, including the Prince, agreed to tolerate certain changes so that the

---

* A most controversial character who left his mark both in Europe and the Americas.

really important things, such as their status, wealth, and power could be preserved. This particular way of conceding a little in order to protect privilege came to be known as "gatopardism," from the original title of the novel—*Il Gattopardo*. Every western language has adapted the word to its own phonic and spelling rules for the simple reason that it describes the undeniable fact that no one in an advantaged position wishes to let go of it.

No doubt gatopardism has yielded excellent social and political results in real life, but it would indeed be interesting to know why many readers of this novel believe that it also succeeded inside the story. It would seem as if they had closed the book halfway through, or as if they were impervious to the many pages that, in fact, tell of a different outcome.

The Prince pretends that nothing is amiss. He holds his head up proudly, and encourages his family to pursue the ancestral ways of the family. He commands, entertains, drinks, and fornicates in grand style, as have done all other Salinas before him. Nevertheless, his sensibility reluctantly grasps the idea that where leopards and lions ruled jackals and hyenas will dwell unchecked. And yet he does nothing to prevent the fall. Perhaps he feels that there is no stopping the wheel once it has started to turn, or perhaps his sense of fatality whispers in his ear that "so it has been written."

Only on one occasion did he openly voice his views about the new order. When offered a seat in the Senate established by the Savoyan authorities, Salina declined the honor conferred upon him. Without abandoning the refined language of a true aristocrat, his refusal enveloped the bitterness of his feelings and contained a slight touch of irony that the government's messenger was unprepared to detect.

> I belong to a wretched generation, astride between the old days and the new [...] What good could I do in the Senate? I am an inexperienced legislator who lacks the ability to deceive himself, an essential requirement to whoever intends to lead the way for others to follow.*

Deep down in his heart, Prince Salina felt torn between his loyalty to the social and political order into which he had been born and the inevitability of *progress*. Convinced that the future would sooner rather than later fall into the hands of the unscrupulous, he took the liberty of suggesting that Calogero Sedàra, an upstart who had been buying land and amassing a fortune in a somewhat shady way, be appointed to represent the region in Parliament.

---

* My translation from the Italian original.

This shocked the envoy off his feet. He protested that, if honest men stepped aside, unprincipled, near-sighted people—the likes of Sedàra—would advance unchecked, and such advancement would mean no more and no less than a return to the kind of feudalism that the reforming party intended to oust under Garibaldi's leadership.

Yet the Prince did not budge, and the matter was discussed no further.

Alongside Salina's internal struggle to come to terms with the forces of history and to adopt a stance with which he felt al least not entirely uncomfortable, Lampedusa did not neglect the flow of private lives in a context of social and psychological upheaval.

In terms of its consequences, the most significant deviation from the backbone of the story describes Tancredi Falconeri's violent passion for Angelica Sedàra.

Practically since her childhood, Concetta Salina, the Prince's eldest daughter, had conceived the hope that she would marry her cousin. Secret and not so secret signs had passed between them, to the point that she requested her father's opinion should he propose to her.

The Prince, an excellent judge of character, dodged the question by asking, in turn, whether Tancredi had already spoken the appropriate words. Upon her denial,

Prince Salina dismissed the issue saying, "We'll cross that bridge when we come to it," or words to that effect.

As it happened, Angelica Sedàra captivated his Sicilian sensuality in a manner that Concetta, being a lady, neither knew how to nor would have debased herself to attempt. In due course, the engagement between the young aristocrat turned revolutionary and Sedàra's ambitious daughter was publicly announced.

One of the Prince's administrators broke the news to him, possessed with such indignation that one could think he had been personally slighted. Prince Salina knew better: far from putting an end to an era, that marriage would mark the beginning of everything that was to come and that he had no power to stop. In fact, his knowledge of the world had taught him that alliances of this kind contributed to the refinement of those who owned the means but lacked all else that good society demanded. "After three generations, artless, uncouth members of the lower middle class (taking as a parameter their manners not their money) become meek aristocrats," he remarked. Not for a moment did he think that the conversion could well work inversely.

Although indisputably focusing on the predicament of the aristocracy embodied by Prince Salina, *The Leopard* does not ignore the unrest of the lower classes or the worries of the Catholic Church. A conversation between Don Pietrino, the Salinas' priest-in-residence, and his friend Father Pirrone best exemplifies what went through the minds of those who watched the so far unthinkable subversion of an ancestral distribution of roles.

> [. . .] If that class [the aristocracy] were to disappear, as has so often happened before,* an equivalent class will arise, with the very same qualities and defects of their predecessors in power.†

In other words, the notion that "If we want things to stay as they are, things will have to change" had taken deep roots in every social sector. Depending on their status, different characters foretold this outcome with relief or with regret.

And yet.

It would be ideal if you could read the novel before going on to the next paragraph which, among other things, includes a comment on the ending.

---

* Father Pirrone was referring to the aftermath of the French Revolution and the revolts in Poland.
† My translation from the Italian original.

Prince Salina suffered the indignity of dying in a hotel in Trinacria, surrounded by "amenities" that, according to his nephew Tancredi, the state of repair of his family home could no longer provide.

In a way, he was relieved to take leave of a world beyond his comprehension.

If we stop to think for a moment, we may agree that many aged people who reach the end of their earthly path with a lucid mind must feel the same. The world they know is long gone, together with the friends and relations with whom they shared values, experiences, opinions, and memories. Nothing must feel more alien to a human being than the certainty of living in an unrecognizable environment, while the younger generations keep repeating that it is exactly the same environment in which the perplexed individual used to feel completely at ease.

At the end of his days, Prince Salina confirmed what he had anticipated and feared after that first moment, when he sincerely believed that nothing would really change if he and others like him went along with the proposals that his nephew so enthusiastically embraced.

Still, his nephew, for example, had yielded to political and financial opportunism. While it is true that he had retained the title of Prince Falconeri, he had done so to enhance his chances of material profit rather than to uphold the virtues of the class in which he had been born and raised.

The youngest generation of the Salina family (the Prince's grandson Fabrizietto by his daughter Chiara) mirrored the worst combination of decadent nobility and self-complacent bourgeoisie. He would have, if anything, a dim recollection of his aristocratic origin, upon which he would look as a sheer accident of fate.

The Prince's three unmarried daughters—for Concetta never overcame the wound inflicted by Tancredi's change of heart and her two other sisters would not marry beneath them as did Chiara—continued to live in the Salina palace, stifling in the mummified atmosphere of what had long been forgotten and replaced outside the thick medieval walls.

You may be a staunch defender of change insofar as it means progress. Well, sometimes it does and others not. More often than you would like to recognize, change, though unavoidable, takes away much that is good and levels downwards. Through a number of changes, many of our societies, of which the one depicted in *The Leopard* is but an example, have achieved a fairer social structure and equality of opportunity ... and have paid a price for it.

Now you have the right to be exploited by the system just as does your neighbor, to fret about your pension and your old age, to squeeze your brains so as to keep one step ahead of inflation (good luck with that!) thanks to the equality brought about by a few changes. Such is the beauty of gatopardism: all must change for everything to remain the same.

I can hear indignant voices rising to remind me of the rights granted to minorities (which, by the way, seem to have grown into majorities: just look around you) and of the fact that cutting edge technology is available to practically everyone.

I know. I also know that there are two things that we do not seem to be able to escape: the designs of the "Masters of the Universe" (and I certainly do not mean He-man and company)* and our own discomfort as we feel robbed of our expectations/dreams.

Many of you will laugh away the above reflection. Remember, then, Prince Salina. Ours is a different time, but a little scraping on the surface will probably show that the differences have not affected the core of a society that has changed denominators and left the essence unscathed.

For further insight into this novel, it would be great if you could find information about/read the following:

---

* See Viviane Forrester's *The Economic Horror.*

Riall, Lucy: *Garibaldi, Invention of a Hero*
Clark, Martin: *The Italian Risorgimento*
History of Sicily: en.wikipedia.org/wiki/
   History_of_Sicily

Kazuo Ishiguro

An Artist of the Floating World

Nothing is more disturbing than the feeling of alienation aroused by otherness. We fear those whose customs, language, and appearance differ so much from ours that we cannot label them except as "The Others." We then tend to perceive them as a threat unless, as is so often the case, the "others" relinquish their uniqueness and adopt our ways. Once this process has been completed, we stop noticing slanted eyes, crooked noses, or dark skins. Thus we may feel horrified that these "others" who are now "not others" may have been subjected to unspeakable humiliation when they were still authentically true to their own roots.

Most of us know of two Japans: the one depicted in Hollywood movies during and shortly after World War II* (a country of barbarians and torturers that deserved the bomb, yes sir) and the present world power, whose

---

* Fortunately, Clint Eastwood showed a different outlook in his film *Letters from Iwo Jima*, after years of struggling with producers who believed that too much water had gone under the bridge for anyone to care.

technological advances and prompt adoption of the occidental way of life brings them so close to us that we can hardly perceive them as anything but equals.

Approving of the bomb has eventually become politically incorrect. I have not heard equivalent regrets for the internment of Japanese immigrants and U.S.-born descendants of Japanese families in American camps through the duration of the war. In fact, even former Chief Justice Warren, who was governor of California at the time and gave the order for his state, seems to have kept silent about this decision to the end of his days.

An Artist of the Floating World is a story about ordinary people in Japan soon after the war was over, with occasional flashbacks to war and pre-war times. Told in the first person by a painter who lost his reputation because of his support of the war effort, the novel contributes masterly insight into the "others" when they were still "others." Learning about everyday life, family, relationships, friendship, power, and politics we come to discover that some of the differences deserve our full respect, and begin to wonder whether the occidentalization of Japan did not mean a great loss in terms of cultural diversity.

Masuji Ono, the now elderly painter, embroiders the novel with his views on art and the role of the artist. If, as one could surmise from the title, Ishiguro intended to draw our attention to the dilemmas that every artist has to face, I'm afraid that this narrative line has taken second place because of the compelling pathos of the life stories he unravels, starting with his own.

Mr. Ono lives in a large house that "received its share of the war damage," so parts of it need repairing or rebuilding, and this he cannot afford to do. The first part of the novel is entitled "October 1948." The narrator tells us that he bought the house some fifteen years before, and that he paid a ridiculously low price for it because the previous owners, who had inherited it from their father but did not wish to keep it, set more value upon honor than upon money. Having checked Mr. Ono's credentials back in 1933, they found him to be the most honorable bidder for the house.

The concept of honor runs steadily throughout the story, but just as in all other countries, it takes on different meanings as time passes and circumstances change. Mr. Ono is either too naive or too upright to acknowledge that what one did in perfect good faith in the past, collecting applause for behaving honorably, has now become dishonorable, a source of shame and repentance. Why? Because the Japanese lost the war, and so everything that looked right must have been wrong, and honor is measured by other standards.

Mr. Ono became an outcast for the simple reason that he did not change sides in time, unlike many of his friends and disciples, who saw what was coming and conveniently distanced themselves from him and the warlike enthusiasm that they too had expressed in life and art when they believed in the possibility of victory. Ono's paintings were removed from the places where they stood on exhibition, and he played the role of scapegoat to the salvation of many who pointed their finger at him as the instigator of their "mistaken notions about the war." He was fortunate that his elder daughter got married just before the war started, but his second daughter, although she never said this openly, was experiencing much trouble in being accepted as a daughter-in-law by a respectable family. No such family—that is to say, no family that, after the war, emphatically denied their pre-war and war period convictions—wanted their modified sense of honor stained by harboring an Ono.

You may think that the issue of family approval is one of these "alien customs" that we Westerners find so quaint. Still, in 1948 no young man of good family dared marry without his parents' consent anywhere in the world. Noriko, the younger daughter who got snubbed because of her father's past public activity and pro-war paintings, vented her frustration on him without daring to broach the matter directly. Setsuko, the elder, attempted subtle approaches to make him aware that, unless he made some *mea culpa* at the coming encounter with Noriko's new prospective in-laws, it was quite likely that her sister would remain forever single. Moreover, apologizing alone would not do the trick. Setsuko practically spelled out that, "to avoid misunderstandings," her father visit some of his past acquaintances before the detectives engaged by the Saito family (Taro Saito was Noriko's new suitor) got to them.*

Mr. Ono did not quite understand what he had to apologize for. However, he grasped what was at stake and made the rounds of his past with various luck. At the *miai*,† the troubled father made a moving statement about accepting that his "was part of an influence that resulted in untold suffering" for the Japanese people. The Saitos did not press him further, and soon Noriko entered their family as Taro's wife.

A couple of points shake the non-Japanese reader's sensibility. One is the impudent way in which Ichiro, Mr. Ono's extremely young grandson by Setsuko, addressed his elders and was encouraged to persist in his forwardness and insolence, for he was thus giving signs of "virility." Another is that this child was completely immersed in Occidental culture, even trying

---

* In those years, the old custom of having prospective in-laws thoroughly investigated still persisted. What puzzled Mr. Ono was that he was well acquainted with Dr. Saito, the young man's father, so it had not occurred to him to dig into the Saitos' past.

† The formal gathering between the families before consent was given or withdrawn on either side.

to repeat the English words and expressions that he heard in films and on TV. Both his parents, but mostly his father, who had fought in the war, celebrated this streak as something utterly desirable. Another kind of behavior, perhaps the one that we find the hardest to swallow, is that several men of Mr. Ono's generation committed suicide by way of atonement for having led the country to a dishonorable war. "Dishonorable" in terms of the outcome, for it stands to reason that if the Japanese had not been beaten to the last man the war would have been "most honorable." Those who, after going back to civilian life, were working under these men, felt that their immolation cleansed them all, that their own individual honor was being restored in these deaths. Thus the ancestral and the new intertwined in a new dimension that, little by little, engulfed much of the genuine Japanese spirit and established the Occidental standards by which the new generations live.

It is up to each reader to decide on the moral aspects of colonization, regardless of the fact that no violence was exerted. Or was it?

It would be ideal if you could read the novel before going on to the next paragraph which, among other things, includes a comment on the ending.

In the end, I am sorry to say that Mr. Ono's closing words summarize his apology to the Saitos into an apology to the world at large. I wonder why Ishiguro saw fit to twist the nature of his main character and narrator to this extent, and will not venture an explanation for his decision. Instead, I would like to dwell for a moment on an aspect of the novel that may be regarded as a great treatise on the tensions between students and teachers.

Although Ishiguro specifically refers to the transmission of art, what he says applies to all other teaching-learning experiences as well. In a nutshell, he posits that a good teacher should be happy when his students either go farther than she has taken them or diverge from the paths that the teacher has dubbed legitimate. And indeed she/he should, for such freedom of spirit proves that the teacher has done a great job, which does not lie so much in instructing the student as in strengthening her wish to make independent choices and stand by them.

Unfortunately, many excellent teachers also have enormous egos. It offends them that a student follow an altogether different path, and they experience a deep narcissistic wound when a student surpasses them in excellence. These teachers feel jealous or betrayed, as the case may be, and are incapable of forgiving the "ungrateful wretch." Not that there is anything to forgive, but this is how they see it.

In life, every adult has been both a student and a teacher, since she has learned from many other people and has taught others, more often than not inadvertently.

The book shows that when these cases of "treachery" occur in an art class, the culprit leaves of her own accord or else is made to leave even if she prefers not to. And when yesterday's beloved face has turned into today's object of hatred, the name attached to it is silenced. For all practical purposes, the transgressor has become an evil ghost whose memory should be erased forever for fear that it may bring misery and ill-luck to the "survivors."

The interesting thing about this behavior is its repetition in other activities that have no connection to art whatsoever. The thoughts and descriptions of the art world in the "floating world" are worth extracting from the main plot to give it very special consideration. For here is where no one can claim "otherness." The bonds that we find in these digressions, as Mr. Ono calls them, lay on the text a coat of universality that makes brothers and sisters of us all.

For further insight into this novel, it would be great if you could find information about/read the following:

World War II : en.wikipedia.org/wiki/World_War_II

Davies, Roger and Ikeno, Osamo: *The Japanese Mind: Understanding Contemporary Japanese Culture*

Iwabuchi, Koichi: *Recentering Globalization: Popular Culture and Japanese Transnationalism*

Wai-Chew Sim: "An Artist in the Floating World" in *Gobalization and Dislocation in the Novels of Kazuo Ishiguro*

Margaret Atwood

The Penelopiad

At first sight, *The Penelopiad* offers Penelope's version of Odysseus's participation in the ten-year long Trojan war and the subsequent hindrances that kept him away from home—and her—for another ten years.

Just in case you do not remember Homer's extraordinarily beautiful poem about the hero's adventures, let me summarize *The Odyssey* in very few words. Ready to come back to his kingdom of Ithaca after the looting and burning of Troy, Odysseus* falls prey to the wrath of Poseidon, lord of the seas, whom he has slighted in more than one way. Resorting to all his cunning and with the help of the goddess Athene, he finally manages to arrive safely home, kill the impudent princes who have been depleting his land while urging his wife Penelope to pick a new husband among them (since it was clear to them that Odysseus had perished

---

* Also known as Ulysses, although they seem to have been two different characters. Since both Homer and Atwood speak of Odysseus, I will stick to this name and you can then find out who was who in the suggested readings at the end of the chapter.

long ago), and execute those of his wife's maids who partnered up with the uninvited, unwelcome guests during the term of his absence.

Thanks to Homer's narrative, the name "Penelope" has become synonymous with "a perfect wife," the kind every man dreams of even if in our times he keeps his thoughts to himself out of political correctness. In fact, the story goes that Penelope ruled Ithaca as would have done the best of administrators, greatly increasing her husband's estate despite the plundering of the suitors. Although she was but a girl when Odysseus left her in charge of his island and their son Telemachus, she never once dreamt of another man, and patiently devised tricks and excuses to postpone the moment of choosing one among the princes, all of this without breaking the rules of hospitality. One could then say that she was an accommodating wife who never shamed her husband in public or in private, and one that was perfectly happy to renounce her sovereign power once Odysseus was ready to come back into his own.

Penelope's protagonism is at least intriguing if we take into account that she appears very briefly in only six of the twenty-four books of *The Odyssey*, and that she is mentioned without much significant detail in some of the others.

Anyhow, in this novel she, addressing the reader directly, tells her own story. You will learn about her thoughts presently, but I would first like to point out that whether or not Margaret Atwood intended to write a book about gender (apparently not), this seems to be precisely what she achieved. By the end of the book she has informed us on the battle of the sexes and the struggles among women for preeminence of some kind, so even if you opt for paying little attention to the myths that keep the plot together, you will have a great time rethinking gender issues.

You meet Penelope in the Underworld. Together with a general description of the afterlife, she takes great care to tear to shreds the Odysseus persona* created by Homer. In her complaints you can recognize many a wife screaming to whomever will listen that the publicly admired husband is not that admirable or worthy, that he has flashed false diamonds all along.

Also, like many other women, she loved him enough to believe that he would not lie to *her*. What she most regrets is, precisely, having been made into the epitome of the perfect wife discussed above. She would like to warn women not to follow her example, but it is too late. The living cannot hear the words of the dead.

---

* A character in literature. In this case, a second meaning is pertinent: the role publicly assumed by the character (in this case, Odysseus) as distinguished from his inner self.

Penelope's biff with Helen of Troy goes on in Hades* just as angrily as it developed when they were alive. Myth depicts them as cousins, with beautiful, haughty Helen always making fun of guileless little Penelope. One might mistakenly suppose that, besides bearing her a grudge for all the snubbing that went on in their childhood and early adolescence, Penelope hated Helen because, in a way, she provoked the war that kept her a grass widow for twenty years. In fact, what irks her about Helen is that, although deprived of a body just as the rest of the dead, she still behaves as if she had one, precisely that body and face that allegedly caused the war.

In *The Odyssey*, Homer takes extra care to pinpoint that Penelope was as beautiful as she was wise, whereas *The Penelopiad* insists, through Helen's vexing comments, that Penelope had no choice but to play wise to make up for her plainness. The eternal battle between the man-eater and the prudent housewife is deployed in every subtle light.

One of the funniest and most touching themes in this novel lies in the contrast between Odysseus's great feats during his struggle against the obstacles in his way and Penelope's pedestrian—and probably true—interpretation of such deeds. In her eminently

---

* One of the names of the Underworld.

practical mind, the divine Circe who, according to Homer, held him captive through sorcery, probably was just a wily, sophisticated, and expensive whore. In other words, Atwood brings the grandeur of one of the most reputed heroes of the Achaean league down to the level of a cheating husband whose wife pretends to believe his lies but knows exactly what is what.

One most intriguing theme that runs parallel to the storyline is the execution by hanging of twelve slave maids, Telemachus's* early playmates and Penelope's eyes and ears among the suitors. In a somewhat Brechtian way†, the maids tell about their lives and complain bitterly that their fate might have been different had they been born into rich families. They blame Penelope as much as they do Odysseus for their death, and will appear with accusing eyes to one or both of them during their strolls in the Underworld.

The author provides an interesting explanation referring to ritual sacrifice in matriarchal times, but supposing you do not wish to pursue the anthropological evidence, you will clearly see that, in those ahistorical times, women were discriminated against by men while establishing differences among themselves on the basis of birth and social status. Whether

---

* Odysseus and Penelope's only son.
† German playwright Bertolt Brecht used to insert songs, poems, and chorus lines in his plays, particularly in the so-called "didactic" ones.

the past is the right tense for the above assertion remains your decision.

In many ways, Penelope resembles the average housewife. She has to cope with an indifferent, not to say unloving, mother-in-law who barely talks to her but does not miss a chance of remarking that "she does not look well." She feels desperate watching her son grow into manhood and confronting her; she cannot refer him to his (absent) father for advice on what still are "men's issues," and needs to keep the kingdom going and thriving single-handed, just as countless women of our times need to run their home, go out to a job, and succeed at both tasks to avoid social and family criticism.

When you think you have reached the happy ending, with the family reunited, there comes yet one more turn of the screw.

It would be ideal if you could read the novel before going on to the next paragraph which, among other things, includes a comment on the ending.

Despite some interesting attempts at reinterpreting mythical issues that Atwood has found obscure in previous writings about this story, the real challenge in this book lies in its association with real life. How many couples manage a compromise through a little calculated blindness on either side?

Penelope knows that, regardless of his bravery in combat, Odysseus was a scheming, restless soul who probably loved her deeply, but who would not renounce other opportunities to "live the life." Apparently, twenty years of wandering did not quench his thirst for adventure. After putting his affairs in order, life at home proved monotonous and predictable. Besides, Telemachus was now a full-grown man who would be delighted to rule in his place while he sailed away on a new voyage.

Depending on how you look at it, Odysseus had either a perfectly good reason to sail away again or a spotlessly concocted excuse to do so. He told his wife that, during his visit to the Underworld, the spirit of the seer Tiresias had warned him that he would have to purify himself from the blood of the suitors that he was to kill and to appease Poseidon once and for all "by carrying an oar so far inland that the people there would mistake it for a winnowing fan." And so he departed, much against his will, he assured her.

In the fantastic Underworld created by Atwood, the souls of the dead have the chance of reincarnation. Thus, Helen, Odysseus, and Telemachus kept returning to the earth, living other lives, and bringing back news of the latest developments of all kinds. Penelope, true to her nature, never came back. Or so she says.

For further insight into this novel, it would be great if you could find information about/read the following:

Homer: *The Odyssey*
Graves, Robert: *The Greek Myths*
Graves, Robert: *Homer's Daughter*
Frazer, Sir James: *The Golden Bough*

Louis Bromfield

Mr. Smith

In his prologue to the novel, Bromfield claims to have received the manuscript from an ex soldier in World War II. Impressed by the contents as well as by the fact that the alleged author died overseas in a suspicious manner, he decided to entitle the work *Mr. Smith* and used his influence to have it published.

We know that the claim of having received or come across a manuscript is a well-known device used by authors to legitimize the authenticity of their own thoughts, and to reduce the fictional element to a minimum so that the reader actually believes in the truth of the narration.

This particular novel is based on the diaries of a Wolcott Ferris, alternating between his life in Oakdale, U.S.A., and his military service in some godforsaken island on the Pacific, an island that, for lack of a name, he calls "the jungle."

The idea of a private diary sounds always attractive. To begin with, such stuff is not meant for publication and thus contains "highly explosive material for private relief." The reader knows this, too, is a fiction, but the temptation to pry into someone else's mind half convinces her that perhaps, just perhaps, the material unfolding before her eyes may be the real thing.

Ferris's first scribblings describe the rich suburb where he has lived all his life. He shows no kindness for the place, the people, or his wife Enid. In his view, they are all, himself included, living the lies told by the advertising agencies hunting for comfort-seekers, only he shows some degree of awareness that the others seem to lack. He strongly emphasizes that their lives are filled with trash, and that social activity is imperative to shun the terror of spending some time with oneself. The dread of silence leads to either endless chit-chat or heavy drinking; still, Ferris maintains that they all have maggots in the mind, and that the purposelessness of these lives is just a way to kill time till death catches up with them.

He feels totally miserable, in contrast to his wife, who thinks that they are the perfect couple. Ferris insists that love is a rare thing, that the ordinary man cannot experience the great romances and passion described in literature and, what is more, supposing he could, it would be deemed dirty and immoral, for "true love is respectable."

Not that the writer of the diary always "knew." He

says that twelve years before the final arrangement of his notes he really SAW himself in the mirror for the first time. The image triggered existential questions such as "Is that you? What are *you*? What do you wish for? Where are you coming from and where will you end up? Why are you here?"

He was unable to provide answers or, at least, satisfactory answers to such questions. He mercilessly blamed the University system and the falseness of placing appearances above substance. This and a couple of other things became what "one could call the American culture and civilization or, more accurately, the lack thereof."

At a time when so many couples were getting divorced, why did Ferris not pursue this option? He tells us that, although deep down and for all her pretence, Enid was just as unhappy as he was (or she would not have popped down sleeping pills like candy), she would never admit to the failure of their marriage, to having made a mistake in the first place. Moreover, he says that, for sundry reasons, not everyone who wants a divorce goes through with it.

Ferris makes a case for the importance of reading. He feels immensely grateful to the one teacher who taught him to read in the way I discussed in the Introduction to the book you are now reading. Because he has taken full advantage of his readings, he posits that the Greeks believe in the three-in-one theory. In fact, according to this belief, each of us is the person that others believe her to be, the person we believe we are, and the person that we actually are.

Well, Ferris had the opportunity of finding out about all three in the course of a love affair that, paradoxically, made him feel alive while nearly destroying him.

Too much shaken by this experience, he joined the Army as the only possible escape from suicide or murder.

Life in the jungle was dreary, pointless, and a great example of how archetypes from different American subcultures managed to stick together despite their profound disagreement about practically everything.

Ferris—now a captain, the officer in command—tried to maintain a precarious equilibrium among the four men under him: a young Jew, a Kansas farmer, a Brooklyn tailor, and a semi-literate racist from Georgia. In a way, the dark, fearful aspects of the surrounding jungle are duplicated in these men.

The futility of their mission also highlighted the distance between the decision-makers and the rank and file. These men had orders to protect cans of food that might or might not be needed by some hypothetical combat unit in case it happened to land on the island. In the meantime, the natives were consumed by infectious diseases, and a few starving Japanese risked their lives in an attempt to steal some food and thus stay alive.

Ferris knew exactly why he was there: joining the Army had been the only reasonable escape from his intolerable life at home and his brutal loss of the love he had eventually found and enjoyed. However, he remarked that a war in which you do not engage in personal combat with your opponent lacked dignity and honor, and foresaw that precisely this type of war would prevail in future. He firmly believed that America would perfect its technological weapons and would still take part in many more wars that would not exactly threaten the country's autonomy.

One day, they learned that the bomb had been dropped on Hiroshima. So it was all over, yet these men, with one exception, did not rejoice at such an ending. And then, when it was time to go back home and try to resume life as it had been before, they started dying. Only one survived, Sergeant Burke, the one with whom Ferris empathized the most. From a literary point of view, Burke was necessary to convey the manuscript to the writer who then had it published. The circle closed. Hell remained entrapped in it, only to break loose again every time *Mr. Smith* finds an attentive reader.

It would be ideal if you could read the novel before going on to the next paragraph which, among other things, includes a comment on the ending.

It is suggested that, in a way, Ferris committed suicide by getting himself killed. Death hovers over the novel, sometimes under its true names, murder and suicide included, and others raising her head from existential questions or reflections about the vacuity and conformity of middle-class life.

You may argue that too many things have changed since the post-war period to give importance to the issues developed in *Mr. Smith*. It cannot be denied, for example, that sexual repression is unknown to the younger generations. On the other hand, living sexual experiences as if one were drinking a glass of water can prove as empty, meaningless, and anguishing as repression itself. You may also argue that divorce as a solution to lives that have driven apart like Mr. and Mrs. Ferris's has become a daily practice, so why make such a big deal of marital incompatibility today? Again, a series of divorces points to a series of failures, and you must admit it hurts. In the first place, most divorces stem from an initial error of judgement at the time of choosing a partner. In the forties and fifties young people had to face social and family constraints at the time of getting married. Most of such constraints are, in fact, a thing of the past, so they had excuses that we cannot flaunt.

Moreover, the difference that Bromfield establishes between "love" and "*l'amour*" is still valid. That people refuse to dwell on the subject will not make it disappear.

In regard to other topics, America has, in fact, got involved in several wars that had little to do with human dignity and much to do with economic interests. When the balance of power changed dramatically after World War II, the average American, no doubt persuaded by the slick hydra-tongues of an invisible superstructure, believed that his/her sacred calling was to save the world. Superman and Wonderwoman may have gone out of fashion as heroes in comics, but they breathe in many American hearts. The question is, save the world from what? To safeguard whose interests? Think on it.

Finally, we can understand the present only if we know and understand the past. Learning what previous generations lived, felt, and thought sheds light on what we read as contradictions or enigmas in our times. The outstanding quality of writers like Bromfield—and the same holds good for the other writers chosen for this book—lies in the fact that they open windows on the lives of men and women that are not you, but could be you.

There are no happy endings. Still, provided you are willing to expand your comprehension as to the why and leave aside the what for one split second, you will experience the sort of happiness that cannot be taken away from you: that of enlarging the scope of your vision no matter how hard evilmongers strive to darken the picture.

For further insight into this novel, it would be great if you could find information about/read the following:

Proust, Marcel: *In Search of Lost Time*
Lewis, Sinclair: *Babbitt*
Mailer, Norman: *The Spooky Art: Thoughts on Writing*

www.ingramcontent.com/pod-product-compliance
Lightning Source LLC
LaVergne TN
LVHW011427080426
835512LV00005B/307